D1384401

Take Note

- Descriptions in this manual are based on default settings of Google Pixel 5a 5G.

- All the instructions in this book is strictly for the use of Google Pixel 5a 5G and not advisable to try it out on any other Google Pixel mobile device.

- Although I made sure that all information provided in this guide are correct, I will welcome your suggestions if you find out that any information provided in this guide is inadequate or you find a better way of doing some of the actions mentioned in this guide. All suggestions should be forwarded to **SodiqTade@gmail.com**.

Copyright and Trademarks

About This Guide

Finally, a detailed guide on Google Pixel 5a 5G is here. This guide is the best for this new mobile device. Spiced with some cool features, tips and tricks with the recent advanced features.

This is a very simple and comprehensive guide, well detailed guide, useful for older adults, experts, newbies and iPhone switchers.

This guide contains a lot of information on Google Pixel 5a 5G and how to use this device like a pro.

It is a step to step guide with screenshots, suggestions and notes. This guide is particularly useful for older adults, newbies and seniors; however, I believe that Pro and experts will find some benefits reading this guide.

Have a wonderful time as you read this detailed guide.

Your gift will be a complete one if you gift this guide together with the new Google Pixel 5a 5G.

Enjoy.

Table of content

Turning Your Phone on/off

Just like many other smartphones, turning on your Google Pixel 5a 5G is as simple as ABC. To turn on your phone, press and hold the Power Key until you notice a small vibration. If you are turning on your phone for the first time, please carefully follow the on-screen instructions to set it up.

Note; It is advisable that you insert the SIM card before switching on your phone.

To insert the sim

- Look for the pin inside the phone box.
- The sim tray is located at the lower part of the left side of your Pixel 5a
- Use the pin into the tiny hole beside the sim tray[apply little pressure] and the sim tray will pop out.
- Gently place your sim card in the sim tray.

To turn off your phone, press and hold the power key and select **Power off.** This will allow your phone to shut down.

As shown below

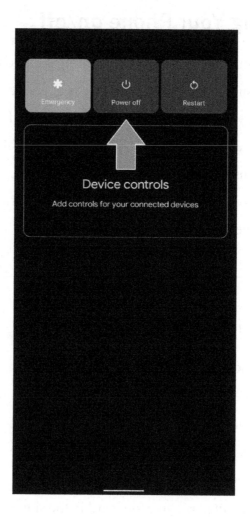

Please do not vex if you find it unnecessary reading about how to on/off your device. I have included it in this guide, in case there may be someone reading this guide who is a complete novice and knows close to nothing on smartphones.

Tips:

- During the setup, you may skip any process by tapping **SKIP** located at the bottom of the screen. Usually, you will have the option to perform this process in the future by going to your phone settings

- Because of software updates, it is likely that your device will consume a large amount of data during the setup, it is advisable that you connect to a wireless network if you can. Using a mobile network during the setup may be expensive.

- You will probably notice that your phone screen locks within few seconds after you finish using it. To allow your phone to stay longer before it locks, change the screen timeout setting. To get this:

  - Swipe down from the top of the screen and select

    Settings icon ⚙ .

As shown below

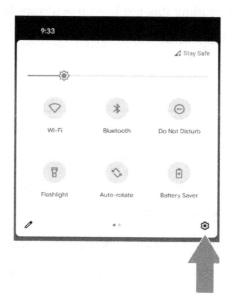

o Tap **Display**.

o Tap on **Advanced**

o Tap on **Screen Timeout**. Then choose any of the options.

As shown below

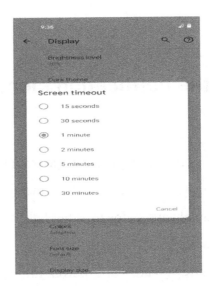

Note: Selecting longer time may make your battery discharge faster. Also it is not really necessary you charge your Google Pixel 5a 5G before the first use. And you can also charge it if there is a way to charge it before the first use.

It appeared that the new lithium batteries used in smartphones don't really need to be charged before first use.

Swiping the Screen Properly

You will need to interact with the screen of your phone by swiping it with your finger time to time. If you don't swipe it properly, you may not get the expected result.

Access the notification menu/quick settings

To access the notification menu, swipe from the top of the screen. Drag down to have full access to more menu on the quick settings panel. You can always swipe to either left or write to navigate through the menu.
Please make sure you are starting from the top of the screen to get the expected result.
As shown below

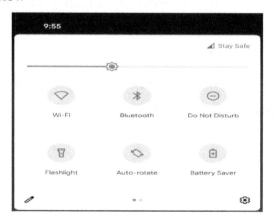

Accessing the app screen

To access the applications screen, swipe up from any part of the screen. See the direction of the arrow below.

As shown below

Settings Tab

Settings tab is one the most used section on every device. And I will be referring to this section a lot.

The settings tab has many subsections, so it is advisable that you use the **Search**  menu to quickly find and navigate what you are looking for. To use the setting's search feature, swipe down from the top of the screen and tap the settings icon.

As shown below

Then tap on the search icon and type a keyword corresponding to the settings you are looking for. For example, if you are looking for settings relating to data usage, just type **Data** in the search bar. As shown below

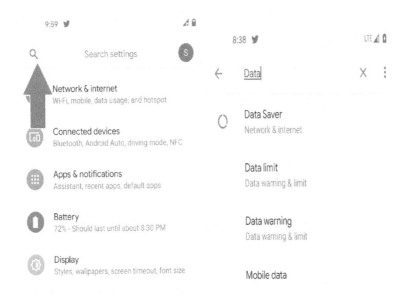

Charge Your Device

It is cool to charge your Google Pixel 5a 5G anytime you are not using it, just to ensure you always have enough power on it. Pixel 5a comes with a better and stronger battery life than the previous Google A series. In case you want to play games, watch videos and do a lot of stuff on it later.

One of the best time to charge your phone is when you are not using it. Maybe when you are taking a nap, in showers or busy with cooking.

To charge your Google Pixel 5a 5G

1. When you unbox, you will notice that the power cord consists of two parts (the USB cable and the power adaptor), connect these two parts together.
2. Connect the end of the USB cable to the charging port of your device, making sure that both the charging cable and the charging port on your device are well fixed.
3. Plug the power adapter to an electrical outlet. When your phone is charging, a charging icon will appear at the top of the screen. When your phone is fully charged, the battery icon will appear full.

4. Unplug when fully charged.

Note: After charging, you may need to apply a small force to remove the USB cord from the phone.

Fast Charging

Your device is built with a battery charging technology that charges the battery faster by increasing the charging power. This feature allows your Google Pixel 5a 5G up to 50% in about 30 minutes. Note: Using your phone while charging may affect the time your phone is going to take to complete a charging cycle.

Inserting and Managing SIM Card

It is important to note that Google Pixel 5a 5G do not support the use of external memory card. I have discussed this in this guide before but this part explains more on how to insert your sim.

To insert memory card or SIM card

1. Locate the SIM and SD Card tray at left edge lower part of the device and gently insert the eject tool/pin included with your phone into the eject hole (located at the left edge) and then push until the tray pops out.
   Note: You may need to apply small force before the tray pops out.
2. Use your hand to pull out the tray gently from the tray slot and place the SIM card on its tray. Please make sure the gold contacts on the SIM is facing up.
3. Slide the card tray back into the slot.

Please note that if the SIM card is not inserted properly, your phone may not recognize it. Make sure you insert the SIM card properly.

Touch screen basics

Your phone's touch screen allows you to easily perform functions and navigate through your device.

Notes*:*

- Do not press the touch screen with your fingertips, or use sharp tools on the touch screen.

- When the touch screen is wet, endeavor to clean it with a dry towel before using it.

These will help protect your touch screen from malfunctioning.

Tips on how to use your touch screen:

Tap: Touch once with your finger to select or launch a menu, application or option.

Tap and hold: Tap an item and hold it for more than a second to open a list of options.

Tap and drag: Tap and drag with your finger, to move an item to a different location in the application grid/list.

How to Lock or Unlock the touch screen

When you do not use the device for a specified period, your device turns off the touch screen and automatically locks the touch screen so as to prevent any unwanted device operations and also save battery.

However, to manually lock the touch screen, press the power key. To unlock, turn on the screen by pressing the power key or double tap on the screen) and then swipe in any direction. If you have already set a lock screen password, you will be asked to enter the password instead of accessing your home page directly.

Rotating the touch screen

You may activate or deactivate screen rotation. To quickly disable or enable screen rotation, swipe down from the top of the screen and

tap .

As shown below

Navigating your device

Google Pixel 5a 5G has two types of system navigation bar.

1. Gesture navigation

As shown below

2. 3-button navigation

As shown below

System navigation allows you to use to manage Home, Back, and Recent buttons or use gestures for more screen space.

By default, your Google Pixel 5a 5G comes with gesture navigation but you can switch from gesture to 3-button navigation.

I will be explaining the two types of system navigation in this guide.

To select between the two types of system navigation:

- Scroll down and tap on **Settings**.
- Tap on search space, and type **System navigation** into the space.
- Suggestions will pop up, tap on **system navigation**.
- Select any of your choice between the two system navigation.

Gesture Navigation

If you are using gesture navigation on your Google Pixel 5a 5G;

- To go **Home**, swipe up from the bottom of the screen.

- To check **Recent Apps**, swipe up from the bottom, hold for 2 seconds, then release.

- To go **Back**, swipe from either the left or right edge

Note: when you swipe either left or right edge, you will get a little direction arrow.

As shown below

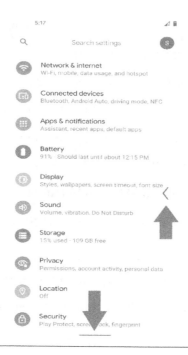

3-button navigation

As shown below

If you are using 3-button navigation on your Google Pixel 5a 5G;

1. To go **Home**, tap on the home button as shown in the number 1 above

2. To check **Recent app**, tap on recent apps button as shown in the number 2

3. To go **Back**, tap on the back button as shown in the number 3

Using the In-APP Back Button

There are some apps that give you the opportunity to go back to a previous screen using the in-app back button ‹ . When available, this button can be found at the upper left part of the screen.

As shown below

The Menu icon

The menu icon is the three dots icon ⋮ that usually appears at the
top of the screen when you open an app.

As shown below

Customize the Home Screen

This allows you to customize your home screen to your taste by switching the widgets, style, wallpapers and a quick touch of home settings.

To customize the home screen to your taste:

- Tap and hold an empty space on the home screen for 2 seconds.

As shown below

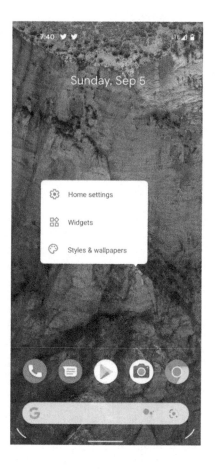

- Tap on **Home settings**

There are couple of settings to do here

As shown below

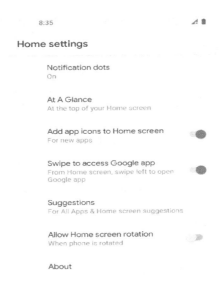

Notification dots

This is a feature that notified you of a notification by adding a tiny

dot on app icon .

To disable this feature;

- Tap on **Notification dots**

- Scroll down and tap on **Advanced**

- Toggle to disable **Notifications dot on app icon**

Also under the **Home settings** you can enable the **Add app icons to Home screen**, **Swipe to access Google app**, and **Allow Home screen rotation**.

Note: These features are enabled by default but you can always these features if you don't want them on your Google Pixel 5a.

To continue with the customization of the Home screen;

- Tap and hold an empty space on the home screen for 2 seconds.

- Tap on **Widgets**

Here you can always add one or two widgets to your Home screen. As shown below

To add widgets to your Home screen;

- Tap and hold the widget you wish to add to your Home screen

To change your Home screen Wallpapers;

- Tap and hold an empty space on the home screen for 2 seconds.
- Tap on **Styles & wallpapers**

Here you can easily change your Google Pixel 5a styles and wallpaper.

- Tap on **styles** to check on more styles.
- Tap on **wallpapers** to check more wallpapers.

As shown below

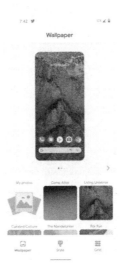

- Tap on any style/wallpaper you want to enable

Add/Remove apps to the home screen

You can add apps/items to the home screen so that you can easily access them anytime you need them.
To do this:

- Access the app screen by swiping up the screen while on the home screen.
- While in app screen, drag the app you want to add to the home screen.
- If you want to remove the app, drag the app to the top left where you have **remove** and release. And you can drag to the top right where we have **uninstall** if you want to uninstall the app. As shown below

Note: Removing an app icon from the home screen does not uninstall the app. The removed app will still be in apps section.

Home Screen Layout:

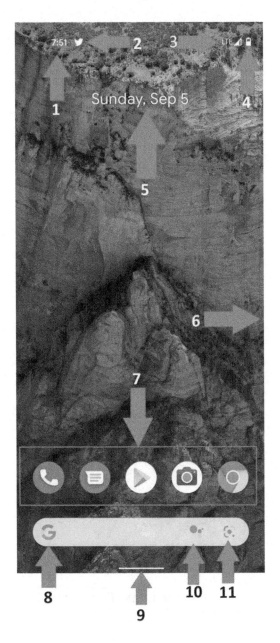

Number	Function
1.	Time space: This is where the time shows.
2.	Notification icon/ Status icons
3.	Sim notification icon.
4.	Battery icon.
5.	Weather widget and daily date updates.
6.	**Back**: Swipe left or write to go back to the previous screen.
7.	**App shortcuts**
8.	**Google search**: This will allow you to run a quick Google search right from the home screen.
9.	**Home Button**
10.	**Google voice assistant**
11	**Google Lens**: To run a quick search on image.

To create a folder on the Home Screen:

From the home screen or application screen, tap and hold an app, then drag and drop it onto another item/app's icon to create a folder.

1. Tap **Edit Name** and enter a folder name.

As shown below

2. To remove an app from a folder, tap the folder, and then tap and hold the app you want to remove and drag it out of the folder to the top left where we have **remove**.

Accessing and Managing Applications

To open an app:

1. From the home screen; swipe up from the bottom of the screen to access application screen.

2. Tap on the app of your choice.

3. To go back to the app grid screen, swipe to either left or right.

Accessing Recently Opened/Running Applications

- Swipe up from the bottom, hold, then release.

- Tap on the app to launch it, or swipe up to cancel/remove the app from recent apps. To close all opened apps, tap **CLOSE ALL** located beside the app screen.

You can also perform some functions with your Google Pixel 5a 5G right from your home screen.

From the recent/running apps we will be talking about;

1. **App info**
2. **Split screen**
3. **Pause app**.

To check this;

- Swipe up from the bottom, hold, then release.

- Tap on the app icon

As shown below

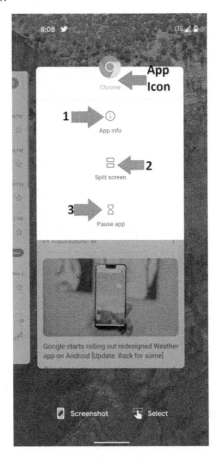

1. Tap on **App info**

Here you will be able to perform some actions like

- **Open the application**
- **Disable the application**
- **Force stop the app**.

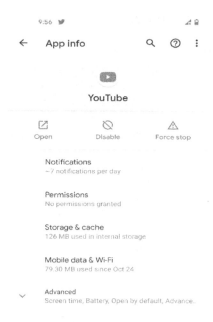

Note: You can disable or force stop an application if the app is misbehaving or freezing.

Right in the app info screen, you can tweak some settings like; the notifications settings, clear cache and storage, check the battery and data usage and many other advanced settings.

2. Tap on **Split screen**

As shown below

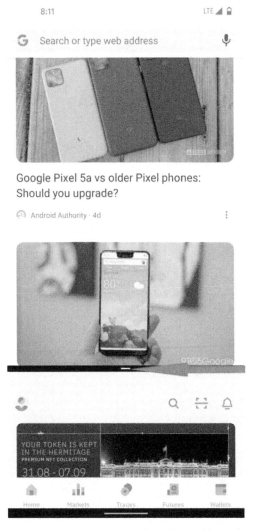

Note; You can always use your hand to adjust the screen of the app by dragging to the particular length. To disable the **Split screen**; drag any app screen to the top.

3. To **Pause app**

- Tap on the pause app

As shown below

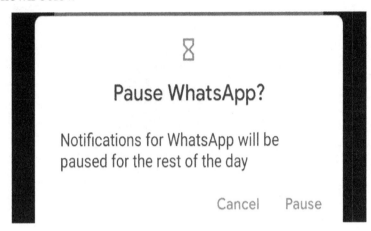

- Tap **Pause** to pause the app.

Quick Toggle Menu

This allows you to have a quick access to great features without having to dig deep into the settings. This is commonly called notification panel because menu you can still view some notifications.

To go to quick toggle menu;

- Swipe down from the top of the screen, swipe again to view more menu

- You can either swipe to left or right to check more features.

As shown below

With just a single tap you can enable the **mobile data**, **location**, **flashlight**, **do not disturb** and many other features.

Edit the quick toggle menu

To edit;

- Tap on the pencil icon

As shown below

Here you can easily rearrange the tiles by dragging each tile into your favourite position.

As shown below

Also you can add more tiles to the quick toggle menu.

To do this;

- Hold and drag to add tiles

You can also reset the quick toggle menu into the default settings. To do this;

- Tap on the 3-dots icon  at the top right corner
- Tap on **Reset**
- Tap on the back icon to go back to the previous screen when you are done editing.

Adjust the screen brightness of your Google Pixel. Drag the slider to adjust.

- Tap to enable any of the features in quick toggle panel and the enabled features would be in blue color.

As shown below

- Tap and Hold on any of the features to go into the full settings of that particular feature. For instance you can tap and hold on the **Bluetooth** to view more about Bluetooth.

Managing Phone Notifications

It is good to know that Notifications consume battery and may be a source of disturbance sometime.

To manage notifications:

1. Tap and hold on the **home screen** for two seconds.
2. Then tap on **Home settings**.
3. Tap on **Notification dots**.
4. Toggle to enable/disable notifications from apps.

As shown below

There are couple of tips you can enable here too.

Notifications on lock screen

This feature allows you to hide silent conversations and notifications.

- Tap on **Notifications on lock screen**
- Select you're the second option depending on your choice.

Sensitive notifications

- Toggle to enable/disable this feature.

Advanced Notification Settings

- Scroll down right in the Notification screen, tap on **Advanced**.
- Toggle to enable/disable

1. **Hide silent notifications in status**
2. **Allow notification snoozing**
3. **Suggested actions and replies**
4. **Notification dot on app icon**

Also you can change some notification sounds under this setting. Note: If you enable **sensitive notification**, it allows your device to show sensitive content when locked. These features are some of the tips and tricks on your Google Pixel 5a 5G that makes the device friendly and more interesting to users.

Bubbles Notification

This feature if enabled allow apps to show bubbles for some conversations. These conversations will appear as floating icons on top of other apps. A form of pop up notifications.

To get this;

1. Tap and hold on the **home screen** for two seconds.
2. Then tap on **Home settings**.
3. Tap on **Notification dots**.
4. Tap on **Bubbles** to enable/disable this feature.

As shown below

By default this feature is enabled.

Note: If you are not interested in bubbles notifications, toggle to disable the feature. This is in case the feature is blocking your view from enjoying other running apps.

Introduction to Settings

- Go to **settings**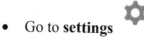

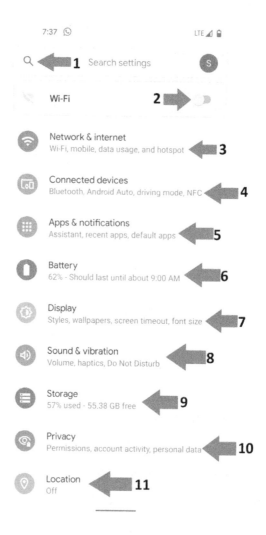

1. Search settings

This allows you to search through the features available on your Google Pixel 5a.

- Type out the feature you are looking for and it will pop up

As shown below

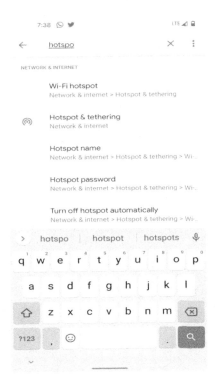

2. Wi-fi

This is another shortcut to enable your device wifi. Wifi enables you to connect your device to other device mobile network.

Note: This will only be possible if the owner of the other device enable their device hotspot.

3. Network & internet

This gives you access to the full settings of **Wifi, Mobile network, Airplane mode, Hotspot, Data saver**, and some other advanced settings,

As shown below

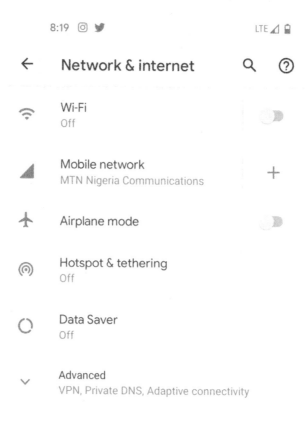

4. Connected devices

This allows you to connect with other devices through Bluetooth. Also you will be able to view your previously connected devices.

- Tap on **See all** to view the previously connected devices

5. Apps & notifications

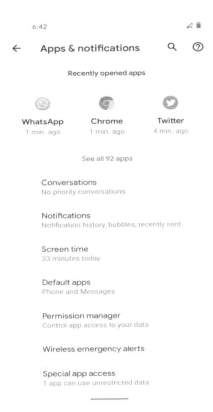

You will be able to check notification history, prioritized conversation, and tweak some other cool features to enjoy your Pixel 5a.

6. Battery

To check more about your Google Pixel 5a 5G battery;

- Tap on **Battery**

As shown below

- Tap on **Battery Saver** to schedule the time you wish to activate the feature.

Adaptive Battery

This feature helps extend battery life based on your phone use.

To extend battery life, adaptive battery may reduce performance and background activity.

- Tap on **Adaptive Battery**

As shown below

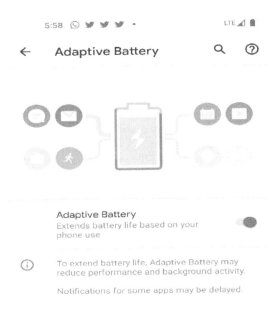

- Toggle to enable this feature.

Note: Notifications for some apps may be delayed.

Battery Percentage

This allows your battery percentage in status bar.

- Toggle to enable this feature.

To check Battery usage

- Tap on 3 dots icon at the top right corner

- Tap on **Battery usage**

As shown below

Note: This will only display the app battery usage. To check the **full device usage**;

- Tap on the 3 dots icon at the top right corner

- Tap on **Show full device usage**

This will show a better and full graphical representation of your device usage together with the app usage.

Lest I forget,

To adjust your volume

Press the **Volume key** up or down, this is the long key located at the right side of your Google Pixel 5a 5G.

7. Display

Display is a subsection of settings with cool features. We will be going through those features one after the other in this guide.

- Tap **Display.**

As shown below

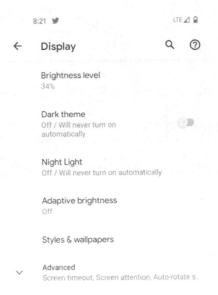

- **Brightness level**

I. Tap on brightness level to adjust your Google Pixel 5a 5G brightness. You can always adjust the brightness from the quick toggle menu as discussed earlier in this guide.

- **Dark theme**

Dark theme uses a black background to help keep your battery longer. Dark theme schedules wait to turn on until your screen is off.

II.   Tap on dark theme to schedule the time you want your device to activate the dark theme.

As shown below

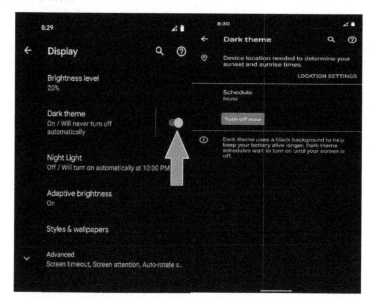

- Toggle to enable the **Dark theme**

- **Night Light**

Night Light tints your screen amber. This makes it easier to look at your screen or read bin dim light, and may help you fall asleep more easily.

III.   Tap on night light to schedule the time you want your device to activate the night light.

As shown below

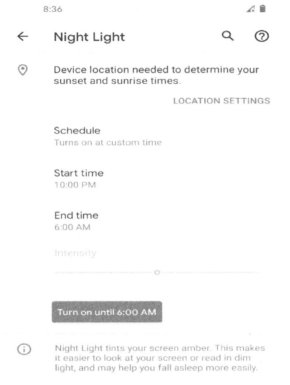

Note: Night light will be automatically enabled whenever it gets to the time you scheduled.

- **Adaptive brightness**

This feature allows your screen brightness to automatically adjust to your environment and activities.

IV.   Tap on adaptive brightness

As shown below

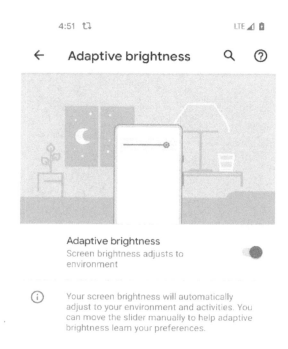

- Toggle to enable this cool feature.

Note: You can always move the slider manually to help adaptive brightness learn your preferences.

- **Styles & wallpapers**
  1. Tap on styles and wallpaper
  2. Tap on your choice of style/wallpaper
  3. Tap on **Apply** to apply the style/wallpaper.

- **Advanced**

This gives you more advanced features on your display. Here we have the **screen timeout** which we discussed earlier in this guide.

We also have some other features like **font size, display size, screen saver, lock screen** and other interesting features.

As shown below

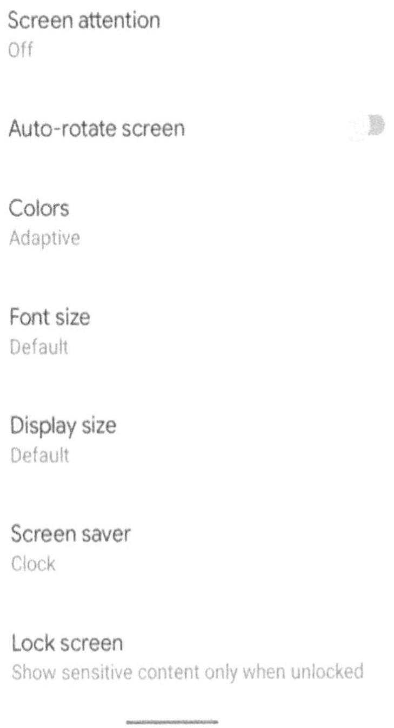

Screen attention
Off

Auto-rotate screen

Colors
Adaptive

Font size
Default

Display size
Default

Screen saver
Clock

Lock screen
Show sensitive content only when unlocked

Screen attention

This is under display advanced settings. It allows you to use the front camera to see if someone is looking at the screen. It prevents your screen from turning off whenever you are looking at it.

As shown below

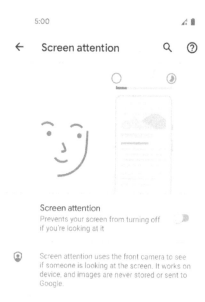

- Tap on screen attention
- Toggle to enable this feature.

Auto-rotate screen
- Toggle to enable this feature

Font size

This feature is also under the advanced display settings. You will be able to adjust your Google Pixel 5a 5G font size here.

- Tap on font size

As shown below

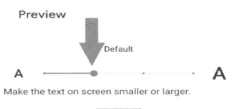

- Drag the slider to adjust the font size from **Default** to **Large** or to **Largest**.

Display size

This feature is also under the advanced display settings. You will be able to adjust your Google Pixel 5a 5G display size here.

- Tap on display size

As shown below

- Drag the slider to adjust the font size from **Default** to **Large** or to **Largest**.

Screen saver
- Tap on screen saver to adjust the settings and change the clock style.

Lock screen

This is a huge feature under the advanced display settings. It has a lot of tips and advanced features that will enable you to enjoy your Google Pixel better.

Under the lock screen, you can enable **Now Playing**, **Tap to check phone**, **Lift to check phone** and other features.

As shown below

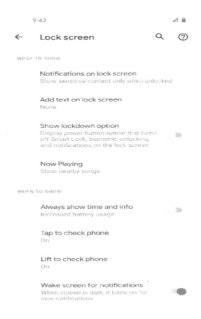

- Tap on **Notifications on lock screen** to change the setting.

- Tap on **Add text on lock screen** to add text to your lock screen.

- Toggle to enable **Show lockdown option**.

- Tap to enable **Always show time info**.

- Toggle to enable **Wake screen for notifications**.

8. Sounds and vibrations

1. Tap **Sound**.

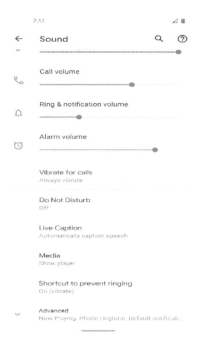

- Drag the slider increase/decrease the volume of the available options.
- Tap on **Vibrate for calls** to set the phone vibration.

Also you can make some tweaks in your sounds and vibration. You can enable **do not disturb, Live caption, Now playing** and some other features. I will discuss some of these features in Tips and Tricks section of this guide.

9. Storage

To check more about your Google Pixel 5a 5G storage;

- Tap on **Storage**

As shown below

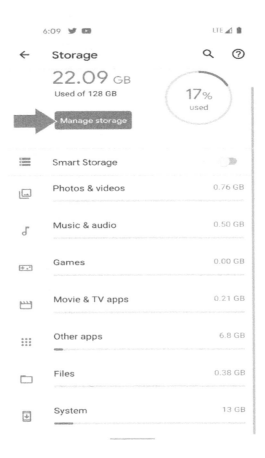

You can also tap on **Manage storage** to clear some redundant files on your device.

As shown below

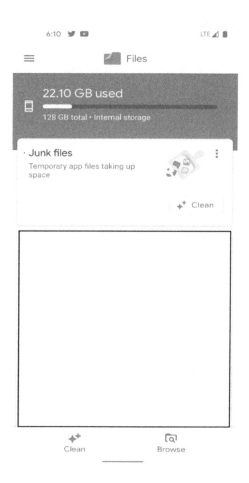

It is advisable to check your device storage once in a week just to clear redundant files and free space for other good files. Although your Google Pixel comes with a large storage capacity.

10.   Privacy

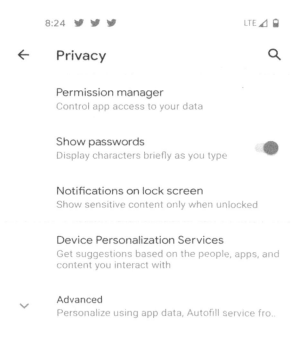

Under the privacy you can adjust **permission manager**, enable **show passwords** and **Notifications on lock screen**.

- Tap on **Advanced** to view more settings under privacy.

11.   Location

Tap and enable location to allow applications access your location.

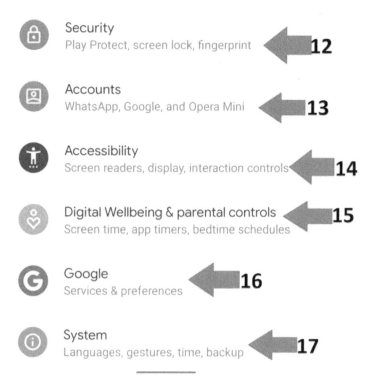

Security
Play Protect, screen lock, fingerprint **12**

Accounts
WhatsApp, Google, and Opera Mini **13**

Accessibility
Screen readers, display, interaction controls **14**

Digital Wellbeing & parental controls **15**
Screen time, app timers, bedtime schedules

Google **16**
Services & preferences

System
Languages, gestures, time, backup **17**

12.   Security

Under security, I will be talking about **screen lock** and **fingerprint** also known as **Pixel imprint**.

To set/change screen lock password or PIN

You can lock your phone by activating the screen lock feature

1. Tap **Security**,

2. Tap a **Screen lock**, then enter your pin and follow the onscreen instructions.

Note: You may choose **Pattern** or **Swipe.** If you don't want a lock screen, tap **None.** Also know you would be asked your password anytime you are trying pen your phone when locked.

To set/add fingerprint

1. Swipe down from the top of the screen and tap Settings icon

 .

2. Tap **Security**,

3. Tap a **Pixel Imprint** , then enter your pin

4. Tap on **Add fingerprint**.

Please make sure you place your fingers properly while registering your fingerprints.

Note: In addition to unlocking your phone, you can also use Pixel Imprint to authorize purchases and app access.

I will still discuss largely on how to name your fingerprints, how to add a finger and how to delete a finger print in this guide.

13.   Accounts

Tap on **Accounts** to view all the register accounts on your device. Accounts like Gmail, Microsoft office, Facebook, Twitter and other accounts you registered on your Google Pixel 5a.

Note: You can also remove accounts you don't want again or accounts you don't use again.

- Tap on the account you want to remove
- And then tap on **Remove**.

14.   Accessibility

Sound Notifications

This feature allows you know what is happening in your home. When Sound Notifications are on, your phone will always be checking for sounds you want to be notified about, like when a smoke alarm beeps or baby cries.

To get this;

- Scroll and tap **Accessibility**
- Tap on **Sound Notifications**

As shown below

← **Sound Notifications**

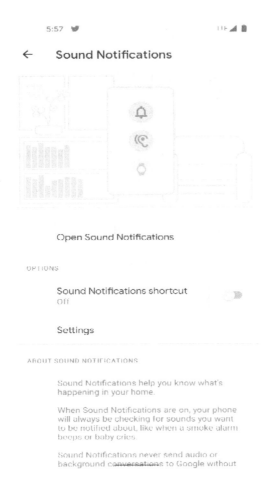

Open Sound Notifications

OPTIONS

Sound Notifications shortcut
Off

Settings

ABOUT SOUND NOTIFICATIONS

Sound Notifications help you know what's
happening in your home.

When Sound Notifications are on, your phone
will always be checking for sounds you want
to be notified about, like when a smoke alarm
beeps or baby cries.

Sound Notifications never send audio or
background conversations to Google without

- Toggle to enable this feature and follow the prompt instructions.

How to use gesture to open Sound Notifications

- Swipe up from the bottom of the screen with 2 fingers.
- To switch between features, swipe up with 2 fingers and hold.

Select to Speak

When select to speak is enabled, you can tap on specific items on your screen to hear them read aloud.

To get this;

- Swipe down from the top of the screen and select Settings

  icon .

- Scroll and tap **Accessibility**

- Tap on **Select to Speak**

As shown below

- Toggle to enable and follow the prompt instructions.

How to use Select to Speak

- Swipe up from the bottom of the screen with 2 fingers.

- To switch between features, swipe up with 2 fingers and hold.

TalkBack

When this feature is on, it provides spoken feedback so that you can use your device without looking at the screen. Talkback is intended for situations or people who have difficulty seeing the screen.

To get this;

- Swipe down from the top of the screen and select Settings icon .

- Scroll and tap **Accessibility**

- Tap on **TalkBack**

As shown below

- Toggle to enable and follow the prompt instructions and tutorials.

How to use TalkBack

- Swipe right or left to move between items

- Double-tap to activate an item

- Drag 2 fingers to scroll

How to turn off TalkBack

Volume Keys: Press & hold both volume keys for 3 seconds.

Note: You can also customize your **TalkBack**.

To do this;

- Tap on **Settings** as identified in the above screenshot.

You will be able to make some adjusts to your device **TalkBack**

Settings. Also it is advisable to take the **TalkBack Tutorials** for

easy learning.

Dark theme

This feature helps turn your screen background theme to dark.

To get this;

- Swipe down from the top of the screen and select Settings

  icon .

- Scroll and tap **Accessibility**

- Toggle to enable **Dark theme**.

Magnification

This feature allows you to quickly zoom in on the screen to display content more clearly. To use this feature, swipe up from the bottom of the screen with two fingers. To switch between features, swipe up with two fingers and hold.

To zoom in:

1. Use shortcut to start magnification
2. Tap the screen
3. Drag 2 fingers to move around the screen
4. Pinch with 2 fingers to adjust zoom
5. Use shortcut to stop magnification

To zoom in temporarily

1. Use shortcut to start magnification
2. Touch & hold anywhere on the screen
3. Drag finger to move around screen
4. Lift finger to stop magnification

To enable **Magnification**;

- Swipe down from the top of the screen and select Settings icon .

- Scroll and tap **Accessibility**
- Tap on **Magnification**

As shown below

• Toggle to enable this feature and follow the prompt instructions.

Color correction

This allows you to adjust how color are displayed on your device.

To get this;

- Swipe down from the top of the screen and select Settings

  icon .

- Scroll and tap **Accessibility**

- Tap on **Color correction**

As shown below

- Toggle to enable this feature

You can toggle to enable **Color correction shortcut** if you are

interested.

Color Inversion

Color inversion turns light screens dark.

To get this;

- Swipe down from the top of the screen and select Settings icon .

- Scroll and tap **Accessibility**

- Tap on **Color inversion**

As shown below

- Toggle to enable this feature

Accessibility Menu

The Accessibility Menu provides a large on-screen menu to control your phone. You can lock your phone, control volume and brightness, take screenshots, and more.

To get this;

- Swipe down from the top of the screen and select Settings icon .

- Scroll and tap **Accessibility**

- Scroll down and tap on **Accessibility Menu**

As shown below

- Toggle to enable this feature
- Tap on **Settings** to enlarge the button.

How to use Accessibility Menu

- Swipe up from the bottom of the screen with 2 fingers.

- To switch between features, swipe up with 2 fingers and hold.

Power button ends call

This allows you to end calls when you press the power button.

To get this;

- Swipe down from the top of the screen and select Settings

  icon ⚙.

- Scroll and tap **Accessibility**

- Scroll down and toggle to **enable Power button ends call**.

Sound Amplifier

This helps enhance audio quality around you and on your device. Sound Amplifier makes weak sounds louder without making powerful sounds too loud.

To get this;

- Swipe down from the top of the screen and select Settings icon ⚙ .

- Scroll and tap **Accessibility**

- Scroll down and tap on **Sound Amplifier**

As shown below

- Toggle to enable this feature and follow the prompt instruction.

How to use Sound Amplifier

- Plug in wired headphones or connect Bluetooth headphones
- Start Sound Amplifier

15.   Digital Wellbeing & parental controls

Focus mode

This feature allows you to pause distracting apps and hide their notifications anytime you need to focus. Maybe you want to read on your device and you don't want to be disturbed you can just enable this feature.

To get this;

- Swipe down from the top of the screen and select Settings

  icon ⚙ .

- Scroll and tap **Digital Wellbeing & parental controls**
- Tap on **Focus mode**

- Tick the box of the apps you want to pause

- Tap on **Turn on now** to enable this feature. You can also schedule this feature.

Note: For an easy you can go straight to the **Quick toggle menu** to enable **Focus mode**.

Bedtime mode

This silence your phone and change the screen to black and white at bedtime.

this feature.

To get this;

- Swipe down from the top of the screen and select Settings icon  .

- Scroll and tap **Digital Wellbeing & parental controls**

- Tap on **Bedtime mode**

As shown below

Note: If enabled, this feature would automatically put on your **Do Not Disturb** and **Grayscale** mode. you can disable this under **Customize**.

Parental Control

This allows you to add content restrictions and set other limits to help your child balance their screen time. This feature is mostly useful for those who are willing to buy this phone for their children.

To get this;

- Swipe down from the top of the screen and select Settings

  icon .

- Scroll and tap **Digital Wellbeing & parental controls**

- Scroll down to **Parental controls**

- Tap on **Set up parental controls**

- Read and tap on **Get started**

As shown below

Follow the prompt instructions as you set up your device Parental Control.

Digital Wellbeing

This allows you to get a full report of the way you use your device daily.

To get this report;

- Swipe down from the top of the screen and select Settings icon  .

- Scroll and tap **Digital Wellbeing & parental controls**

As shown below

You can tap on the diagram to view the **Dashboard** OR Tap on **Dashboard** to view more reports.

16.   Google

Here you will be able to view all google services and preferences.

17.   System

Language & input

You can get more done with your phone by customizing it to match your preference language.

To change your language

1. Swipe down from the top of the screen and select Settings

    icon 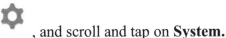, and scroll and tap on **System.**

2. Tap **Language and input.**

3. Tap **Languages**.

4. Tap on **Add language**

To Remove a language

5. Tap on the 3 dots icon 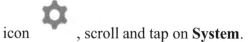 at the top right corner
6. Tap on **Remove**, and tick the language you want to remove.
7. Tap **Remove** to confirm.

Customizing the Default Keyboard

1. Swipe down from the top of the screen and select Settings icon ⚙ , scroll and tap on **System**.
2. Tap **Language and input.**
3. Tap **On-screen keyboard** and then choose a keyboard.

As shown below

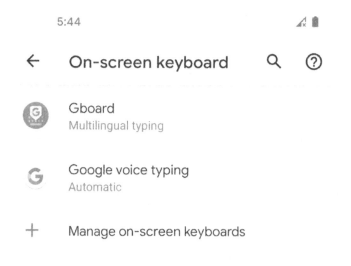

4. Tap on **Gboard**.

Note: If you have not downloaded extra keyboards from Google Play, you may just see only **Gboard** option. Go to Google Play to download keyboard of your choice. Follow the same procedures to change your keyboard to the downloaded keyboard.

Here you will be able to customize your Google Pixel 5a 5G default keyboard.

As shown below

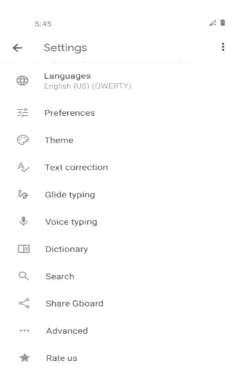

You can change the keyboard theme;

- Tap on **Theme**

As shown below

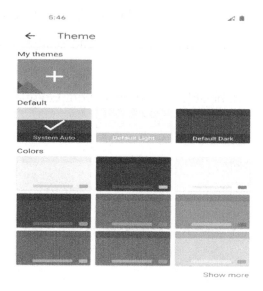

Also you can change keyboard language, preferences, enable text correction, add dictionary and enable some other features that will help you enjoy your device typing experience.

Set the current time and date

Your device is built to update its time automatically, but you may need to manually set your time for one reason or the other.

To set time and date:

1. Swipe down from the top of the screen and select Settings icon ⚙ , scroll and tap **System** .
2. Tap **Date and time**.

Note: You can enable the Use 24-hour format if you prefer it to the regular time format.

Note: In this section of the guide, I have discussed most of the features in settings. Literally, we have 17 sections under settings with many subsections. I will be talking about the other subsections in the cause of this guide.

Some other features under settings are **About phone**, and **Tips & support**.

In case you want to read about your device, just tap on **About phone**, and **Tips and supports** to read more about your device.

Camera and Video

Using the Camera

Both Google Pixel 5a 5G come with rear-facing camera, front-facing camera and LED flash. With these cameras, you can capture a photo and record a video. Although the Google Pixel 5a comes with a single rare-facing camera, the Pixel 5a 5G comes with three rare-facing camera.

Note: Swipe down on the camera screen to view the settings.

Camera layout

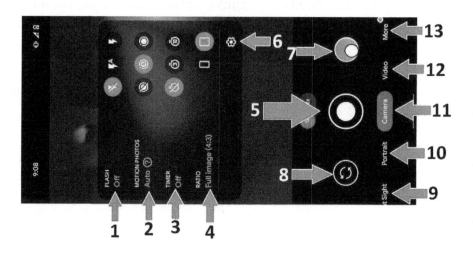

Number	Function
1.	LED Flash button
2.	**Motion photo**.
3.	**Timer**
4.	**Ratio**
5.	Camera shutter/button.
6.	Camera settings.
7.	Preview thumbnail tab.
8.	Front-facing/rear-facing camera switch.
9.	**Night Sight**
10.	**Portrait**
11.	**Camera tab**
12.	**Video tab**
13.	**More** to view more camera options.

To quick launch camera:

1. Swipe down from the top of the screen and select Settings icon

 .

2. Scroll and tap **System.**

3. Tap **Gestures** and tap **Quickly launch camera**.

As shown below

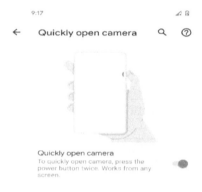

4. Toggle to enable this feature.

This allows you to launch the camera from any screen by double tapping the power key. This feature is enabled by default.

How to record a video

1. When the phone is locked, double-press the **Power Key** to launch the camera app. This is after you've enabled the quick launch camera.

2. Swipe to the video tab then pap on **video button** to start recording.

3. To zoom in while recording, place two fingers on the screen and spread them apart. To zoom out, move the two fingers closer together.

4. To stop the video, tap the **video button** again.

6. To view your recorded videos, go to **Gallery/Photos** app.

How to take screenshot on your device

This allows you to take a screenshot of your device screen. It allows you to capture everything on your display screen.

There are three ways to screenshot. These are:

- Press and hold the Volume down key and the Power key simultaneously until you see it captured the screen. You can edit the screenshot as the option would be displayed immediately after the screenshot.

You can also take screenshot through Google Assistant

- Just say **ok Google take the screenshot**

OR

- Go to recent app screen
- Tap on screenshot

Note: You can also do a couple of stuff when you are done with the screenshot.

- Tap on **edit** to crop and filter the screenshot.

You can **share** the screenshot with friends when you are done editing.

Select

You can also tap on **Select** to copy words from a particular screen.

- Tap on select as identified in the above screenshot
- Tap and hold on the words/items you want to copy.

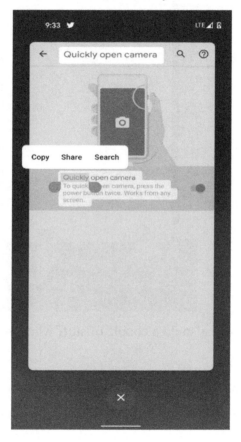

- Tap the **x** to cancel **select**.

Entering a text and More about keyboard

You can enter text by selecting characters on the virtual keypad or by speaking words into the microphone through the use of voice command.

Also you can do more with your keyboard by sending Gifs, Emoticons and other customized texts.

Keyboard Layout

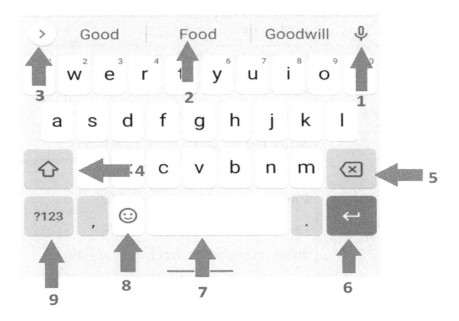

Number	Function
1.	**Voice input**: Enter text by voice
2.	**Predictive text bar:** As you type, your phone will give you text suggestions, the most likely suggestions will appear on the middle space in the predictive text bar.
3.	**Options bar**: Tap to see more options on your keyboard (such as Search, Translate, Clipboard and other options).
4.	Change case
5.	Clear your input/backspace
6.	Start a new line. At times, it serves similar function with Enter as we have it on PC.
7.	**Space bar**: to create space in between texts while typing.
8.	**Emoticon/GIF**: Tap this to add emoticons/GIF to your texts. There different emoticons depending on your mood. This helps make chats more interesting.
9.	Switch between Number/Symbol mode and ABC mode

Note: By default, the following icon would display on top of your virtual keyboard.

1. **Options bar**: Tap to see more predictive texts.

2. **Stickers**: Tap this to get more stickers.

3. **Emoticon/GIF**: Tap this to add emoticons/GIF to your texts. There different emoticons depending on your mood. This helps make chats more interesting and lively.

4. **Clipboard**: You get to see recently copied items in the clipboard. This makes copy and paste easier while chatting.

5. **Keyboard settings:** Tap this to access the keyboard settings.

6. **Options menu:** Tap on the menu bar to get more options

7. **Voice input**: Enter text by voice.

When you tap on the **Options menu**, you get to see this;

Right from here you can adjust some of your keyboard settings. Like you can change the keyboard theme, switch your keyboard to one-handed and some other settings.

How to copy and paste a text

If you are using an app such as Google and you want to copy a link/word from another app to the particular app, this is how to copy and paste:

- Tap and hold a word to display copy options.

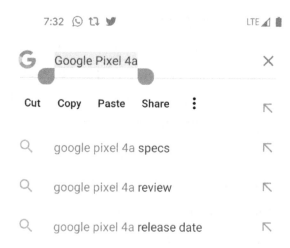

1. If the texts are much drag ![] or ![] to select more texts.
2. Select **Copy** to copy, or select **Cut** to cut the text. Also you can tap on the three dots icon to check out more options.
3. Go to the other app you intend to paste what you've copied, tap and hold on the text space.
4. Select **Paste** to insert the text you've copied.

Note: All recently copied items would be saved in the clipboard. Tap and hold on the text space then tap on **paste**.

- Tap on **Clipboard** to access more recently copied items.

Voice typing option:

- Swipe down from the top of the screen, and tap **Settings**

- Scroll, tap on **System** and then tap on **Languages & input**.
- Tap **On-screen keyboard** and tap **Google voice typing.**

Then use the various options to customize it.

As shown below

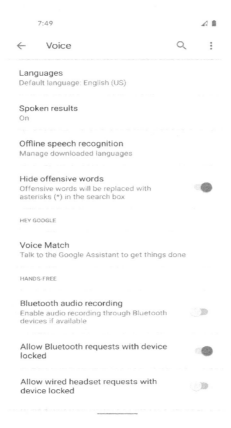

Using the Pixel Imprint Features

One of the interesting features on Google Pixel 5a 5G is Pixel Imprint also known as fingerprint on other android devices. It allows you to unlock applications without going through the stress of entering your passwords. I have briefly discussed about this earlier in this guide nut this time we are going a little deeper into Pixel Imprint.

How to register your Pixel Imprint

You will need to first register your fingerprint before you can use it. You have the chance of registering more than one fingerprint.

Note: You will be asked to set password that will serve as a backup for the fingerprint in case your device fingerprint sensor misbehaves. To do this:

1. Swipe down from the top of the screen and select Settings

    icon ⚙ .

2. Tap **Security**,
3. Tap on **Pixel Imprint** under the **Device Security**
4. Enter your pin and set your **Pixel Imprint**

5. Place one of your fingers on the fingerprint reader located at the back part of the phone then lift it when the fingerprint is detected and read. You may need to repeat this for a number of times.

Easy way to rename Pixel Imprints

1. Swipe down from the top of the screen and select Settings icon .

2. Input **Add Fingerprint** in the search space. Also you can go to **Security**, then tap on **Pixel Imprints**. You will have the same result.

3. Tap on the result, and input your password to unlock.

4. Tap the fingerprint you want to rename. For example, tap **Finger 2.** Tap **ok** to confirm the new name you entered.

As shown below

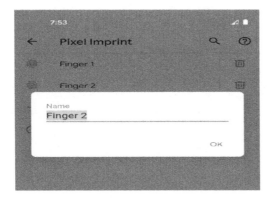

In addition to unlocking your phone, you can also use Pixel Imprint to authorize purchases and app access and can also be used to access bank apps on your phone.

How to delete Fingerprints

1. Swipe down from the top of the screen and select Settings icon .

2. Tap **Security**

3. Tap **Pixel Imprint**.

4. Unlock the screen using your password.

5. Tap on the delete icon 🗑 , and then tap **Delete**. As shown below

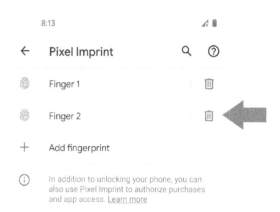

Google Assistant Settings

This feature allows you to do some settings on your Google assistant. Here you will be able to change or add language, set routines, and many other settings.

To get this;

- Swipe down from the top, tap on **settings**

- Input **Assistant Settings** into the search space

- Tap on **Assistant Settings**

As shown below

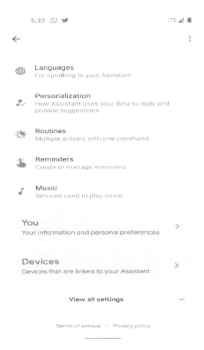

- Tap on **View all settings** to check out more settings.

Note: Make sure your network is connected while doing this for easy connection with the Google assistant. It requires a good network.

Using the Internet App

Opening the Internet browser

We will be using Google Chrome layout in this guide.

To access Google Chrome

- Tap on the **Google Chrome**  .

- Tap **Chrome** On Home Screen If you are using the Internet app for the first time, then follow the instructions.

Note: There are different internet browser. Such as Opera Mini, Mozilla firefox and others

Get to know the Internet Browser Layout

The following are the internet browser[Google Chrome] icons;

Number	Function
1.	**Home:** Tap this icon to go to the browser's home page. The default home page is Google. Tap and hold the Home icon and then select **Other.** Then enter the website of your choice (e.g. Amazon.com) and tap **OK** to add web sites to your browser home.
2.	**Tabs:** Tap this icon to navigate between different webpages you have opened. **Bookmark:** Tap this icon to bookmark. This icon will be marked in yellow color.
3.	**Menu icon:** Tap this icon to access additional options such as **Downloads**, **History** and others.
4.	**Back:** Tap this icon to revisit the most recent page.
5.	**Bookmark icon**: Tap to bookmark a current page. To check bookmarked pages, tap on **Bookmark**.
6.	**Download**: Tap on this to dow nload a page. To chek the downloaded pages and downloaded items, tap on **Download**.
7.	**Info icon**: Tap to view info about running site.

8.	**Refresh:** Tap this icon reloads a webpage.

Note: You can directly access some other features on your internet browser when you tap on the 3 dots icon at the top right corner.

As shown below

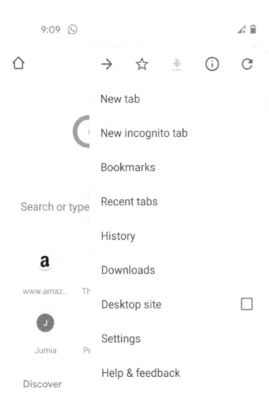

You can access the **History**, **Settings**, **Downloads**, **Bookmarks** and others when you tap on the 3-dots icon.

Phone

Learn how to use your phone app. You can use it to save contacts, make calls and some other call related features.

To make a call or silence a call

While on the home screen, tap **Phone**  and enter a phone number. If the keypad does not appear on the screen, tap the **keypad**

icon to show the keypad.

- To call a number on your contact, tap the **Contact** icon on the Phone app screen. And to call a recent dialed number, tap on **Recent** or **Favourites**.

As shown below

☆   ◷   ዳ
Favorites   Recents   Contacts

- To make a phone call, tap a contact and then tap the phone

icon .

As shown below

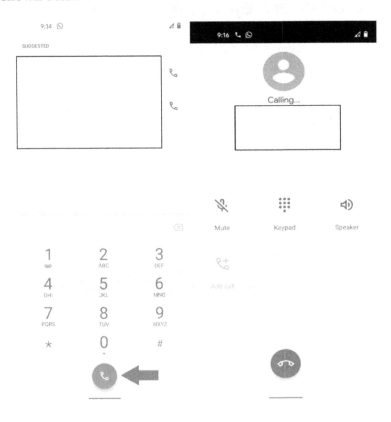

To answer/reject an incoming call:

1. To receive an incoming call, swipe up the **Green phone icon** .

2. To decline an incoming call, swipe down **Green phone icon** .

3. To reply with a text, tap on **Reply** and then follow the prompt instructions.

As shown below

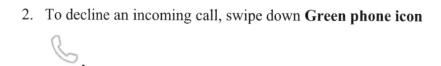

Call from

Reply

Swipe up to answer

Swipe down to reject

Phone Setting

- While on the home screen, tap **Phone**

- Tap on three dots icon located at the top right corner.

As shown below

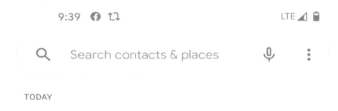

- Tap on **Settings**

As shown below

You will be able to manage call settings, adjust sounds and vibration, block numbers and some other phone settings right under the settings.

Block numbers

This allows you to block calls and messages from specific phone numbers.

- While on the home screen, tap **Phone**
- Tap on three dots icon located at the top right corner then tap on **Settings**.
- Tap on **Blocked numbers**
- Tap on **Add a number** to add a contact to your block list.

There is an interesting tip here that can help secure your device more as shown in the above screenshot.

- Toggle to enable **Unknown** to block calls from unidentified callers.

Note: You wont receive calls or texts from blocked numbers.

Call alerts and ringtones

- While on the home screen, tap **Phone**

- Tap on three dots icon located at the top right corner then tap on **Settings**.

- Tap on **Sounds and vibration**.

- Scroll down, tap on **Advanced**

As shown below

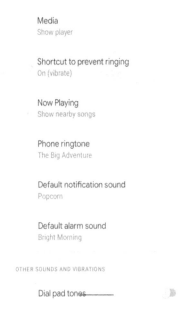

- Tap on **Phone ringtone**

Here you will be able to make some tweaks to your call alerts and ringtones settings.

Display over other apps

This allows apps to display on top of othr apps you are using. This app will be able to see where you tap or change what's displayed on the screen.

For instance, in the screenshot below, the call is displayed over the running app because the **display over other apps** has been enabled for **Phone**.

As shown below

To get this;

- Swipe down from the Home screen, go to **Settings**
- Tap on **Apps & notifications**
- Tap on **Advanced**, and then tap on **Special app access**
- Tap on **Displayed over other apps**

Here you will be able to **allow and disallow** apps. If you want to allow Phone call to display over other apps,

- Tap on **Phone**

As shown below

- Toggle to allow.

Note: Under **Special app access** you can do a couple of things like battery optimisation, notification access, install unknown apps amongst other features.

How to use the Messaging app

This app allows you to send text, photo, and video messages to other SMS and MMS devices.

To start or manage a conversation:

1. Tap the **Messages** app icon from home screen.

2. Tap the **Start chat** located at the bottom right corner of the screen.

3. Type in the first letters of the recipient's name. Your device filters as you type. Then tap the required contact.

Note: You can add up to 20 contact (if not more). If you don't have the number in your contact tap on the dial icon to type the number, To remove a contact from the send list, just tap and hold on the contact, and tap on **x icon**.

4. Tap the text space to write your message.

5. To attach a file such as audio, pictures, tap any of the icons and follow the prompts.

6. When you are done, tap icon

7. Tap and hold message text, and then tap on the 3-dots icon at the top right corner to forward and share a message.

8. Tap and hold the message text to **Delete** the message.

Message Settings

To go to Message settings:

1. Tap the **Messages** app icon 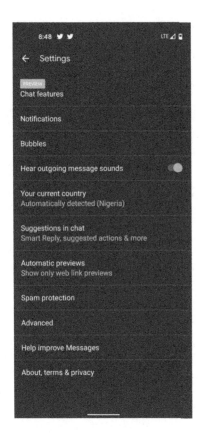 from home screen.

2. Tap on the 3-dots icon at the top right corner, and tap on **Settings**.

As shown below

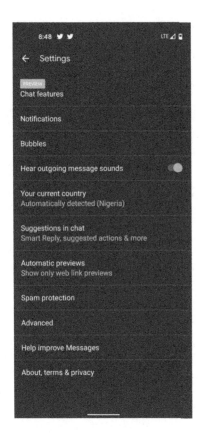

You can make some tweaks on your message settings.

Contacts

This app allows you to create, manage and save a list of your personal or business contacts. You can save names, mobile phone numbers, home phone numbers, email address, and more.

To create a contact:

1. While on the home screen, swipe up and tap on  **Contact** app.

2. Tap on **Add contact** icon located at the lower right corner of the screen.

3. Tap to select where you wish to save the contact.

As shown below

4. When you are done filling the necessary information, tap **Save** located at the top right corner of the screen. OR you can tap on **Discard** if you are no longer saving the contact.

Note: To easily search for a contact, open the contact app and tap **search** bar located at the top of the screen, and type the contact name.

To manage a contact:

1. Tap on **Contact** app 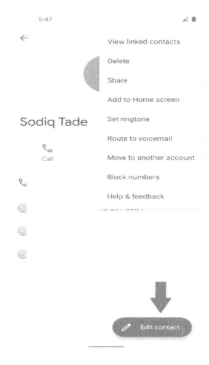 .

2. Tap on a contact from the list.

3. Tap on **Edit** to edit the contact.

As shown below

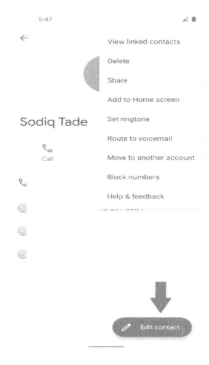

- Tap on 3-dots icon at the top right corner to perform some other actions like share contact, delete, set ringtone, block number and couple of other settings.

Contact Settings: Import or export contacts

If you have some contacts stored on your SIM card, you can move them to your phone or emial vis-à-vis.

How to do this:

1. Tap on **Contact** 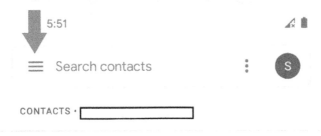 app.
2. Tap menu icon at the top left corner

As shown below

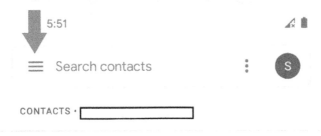

3. Tap on **Settings**
4. Scroll down, tap on either **import** or **export** under **Manage contacts**.
5. Follow the prompt instructions to import/export contacts on your device.

Note: You can Restore, Undo changes, and block contacts here. All under **Manage contacts**.

Do Not Disturb

This feature allows you to mute all calls, alerts, and media, except for your selected exceptions. Also it gives the opportunity to prevent unnecessary disturbances from your phone.

To quickly access this feature:

- Swipe down from the top of the screen using two fingers and then tap and hold **Do Not disturb.**

As shown below

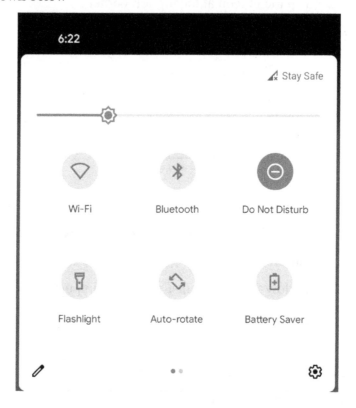

- Tap on **Turn on now** to enable the feature. If you choose to schedule this feature, tap on **Schedules** and follow the instructions.

As shown below

Note: You can follow other options to customize your **Do not disturb.** You can limit the Do Not Disturb feature to a certain people. You can also exempt some apps from this feature.

Connect your device to PC

Your phone can be connected to a PC with USB cable. This will enable you to transfer files such as audio files, document files and image files to your phone from your PC.

Note: You may need to buy a USB cable that works for your PC because the USB cable that comes with your Google Pixel 5a 5G might not work directly with your PC.

Warning: Please not disconnect the USB cable from a computer while the device is transferring or accessing data. This may result in data loss or damage to your phone.

Transferring file with USB

1. Connect your device to a PC with an appropriate USB cable.
2. Swipe down, and tap on **Android system**

As shown below

3. Tap on **File transfer/ Android Auto**.

As shown above

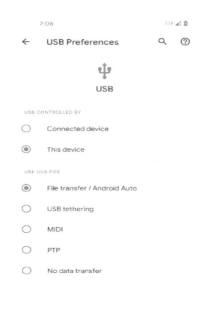

Your Google Pixel 5a 5G should appear in the same location as external USB drives usually appear. For Windows users, this is typically under "This PC/Computer" menu.

1. Open your device's drive so as to see the different folders present.

Note: You may not be able to access the folders if your phone is locked.

Connectivity

Wi-Fi

Using your phone, you can connect to the internet or other network devices anywhere an access point or wireless hotspot is available.

To activate the Wi-Fi feature:

1. Swipe down from the top of the screen.

2. Tap and hold the **Wi-Fi** 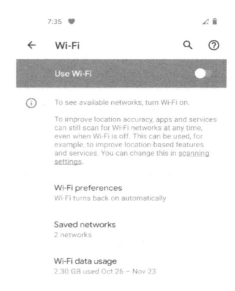 icon.

3. Tap the switch next to Wi-Fi to turn it on.

As shown below

4. Your device then automatically scans for available networks and displays them.

5. Select a network and enter a password for the network (if necessary). If connected the icon will be displayed on your screen.

6. To turn Wi-Fi off, swipe down from the top of the screen,

Tap **Wi-Fi** 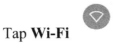 .

Mobile Hotspot

If your network provider support it, you can use this feature to share your mobile network with friends.

1. Swipe down from the top of the screen.

2. Tap on **Hotspot**.

3. Tap and hold **Mobile Hotspot** to access its' settings.

Here you will be able to set the password and do some other settings to secure your network.

Nearby Share

If the receiver device support it, you can use this feature to share your files and documents with friends.

1. Swipe down from the top of the screen.
2. Tap on **Nearby Share**.
3. Tap and hold **Nearby Share** to access its' settings.

Here you will be able to set the password and do some other settings to secure your network.

Using Bluetooth

1. Swipe down from the top of the screen.

2. Tap on **Bluetooth** .

3. Tap and hold **Bluetooth** to access its' settings.

Here you will be able to pair/connect with other device or PC and share files, audio with friends.

Location

Enabling location service allows Google Map, Google apps and some apps to serve you content and make your location visible.

1. Swipe down from the top of the screen.
2. Tap on **Location**.
3. Tap and hold **Location** to access its' settings.

Here you will be able to do some other settings.

Tips and Tricks

Swipe fingerprints for notifications

This allows you to check your notifications, swipe down on the

fingerprint sensor on the back of your phone.

To enable this;

- Swipe down from the home screen, go to **Settings**

- Scroll, and tap on **System**

- Tap on **Gestures**

- Tap on **Swipe fingerprints for notifications**

As shown below

- Toggle to enable this feature.

Flip camera for selfie

This allows you to switch in and out of selfie mode in Google Camera, double-twist when you're in the app.

To get this;

- Swipe down from the home screen, go to **Settings**

- Scroll, and tap on **System**

- Tap on **Gestures**

- Tap on **Flip camera for selfie**

As shown below

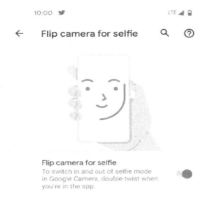

10:00

← Flip camera for selfie

Flip camera for selfie
To switch in and out of selfie mode in Google Camera, double-twist when you're in the app.

- Toggle to enable this feature.

Tap to check phone

This allows you to check time, notifications, and other info whenever you tap your screen.

To get this;

- Swipe down from the home screen, go to **Settings**
- Scroll, and tap on **System**
- Tap on **Gestures**
- Tap on **Tap to check phone**

As shown below

- Toggle to enable this feature.

Lift to check phone

This allows you to check your time, notifications, and other info whenever you pick up your phone.

To get this;

- Swipe down from the home screen, go to **Settings**

- Scroll, and tap on **System**

- Tap on **Gestures**

- Tap on **Lift to check phone**

As shown below

- Toggle to enable this feature.

Prevent ringing

This allows you to prevent your phone from ringing when you press and hold power key and volume up key together.

To get this;

- Swipe down from the home screen, go to **Settings**
- Scroll, and tap on **System**
- Tap on **Gestures**
- Tap on **Prevent ringing**

As shown below

- Toggle to enable this feature.

Flip to Shhh

This allows you to turn on **Do Not Disturb** when you place your phone face down on a flat surface. You will feel a subtle vibration when **Do Not Disturb** turns on.

To get this;

- Swipe down from the home screen, go to **Settings**
- Scroll, and tap on **System**
- Tap on **Gestures**
- Tap on **Flip to Shhh**

As shown below

- Toggle to enable this feature.

Now Playing

This feature allows your Google Pixel to recognise and save background songs with titles in your **Now Playing history**.

To get this;

- Swipe down from the home screen, go to **Settings**
- Scroll, and tap on **Display**
- Scroll and tap on **Advanced**
- Scroll and tap on **Lock screen**
- Tap on **Now Playing**

As shown below

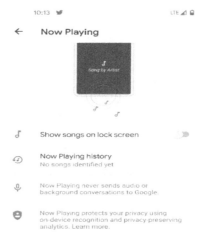

- Toggle to enable this feature

Note: Now Playing will never send audio or background conversations to Google. Now Playing protects your privacy using on-device recognition and privacy-preserving analytics.

Under the **Lock screen**, you can enable

- **Always show time and info**
- **Wake screen for notifications**.

Note: This two features tend to consume battery when enabled.

Live Caption

Live Caption detects speech on your device and automatically generates captions.

To get this;

- Swipe down from the home screen, go to **Settings**
- Scroll, and tap on **Sound**
- Scroll and tap on **Live Caption**

As shown below

- Toggle to enable this feature

How to use Live Caption

- Touch and hold the captions to move.
- Double-tap the captions to expand.

You can also enable **Live Caption in volume control** for easy access to **Live Caption**.

Note: When speech is captioned, this feature uses additional battery. Also all audio and captions are processed locally and never leave the device. Currently available in English only. Songs are not fully supported. And Live Caption for calls is'nt intended for calls with more than 1 other person.

Multiple users

This feature allows you to share your phone by adding new users. Each user has a personal space on your phone for custom Home screens, accounts, apps, settings and more.

To get this interesting feature;

- Swipe down from the home screen, go to **Settings**
- Scroll, and tap on **Sstem**
- Tap on **Advanced**
- Tap on **Multiple users**

As shown below

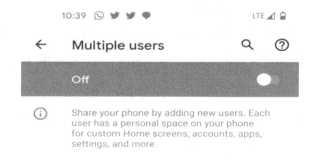

- Toggle to enable this feature

As shown below

- Tap on **Add user** to add more users.
- Tap on **Guest** to **Switch to Guest** or **Remove guest**.

Mutliple users is a great feature that comes with your Google Pixel 5a 5G. You can always follow the same procedures to add users, remove users and switch accounts.

Change your device name

To change your device name:

- Swipe down from the top of the screen and select Settings icon .

- Scroll down, tap on **About phone**.

- Tap on **Device name**.

- Tap **OK** when you are done typing the name.

Colors

This allows you to customize your Google Pixel 5a 5G color.

To get this:

- Go to **Settings**
- Tap on **Display**
- Tap on **Advanced**
- Tap on **colors**
- Tap to select either **Natural**, **Boosted**, or **Adaptive**.

As shown below

App pinning

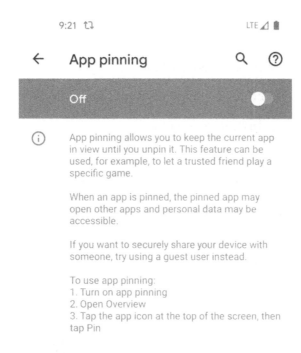

App pinning allows you keep the current app in view until you unpin it. This feature can be used for example, to let a trusted friend play specific game.

To get this:

- Go to **Settings**
- Scroll, and tap on **Security**
- Tap on **Advanced**
- Tap and toggle to enable **App pinning**.

How to use Google Play

Google Play allows you to download apps for your device.

To get this;

- Tap on the Google Play app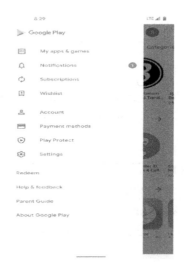

- Search for the app you want to download in the search space

- Tap **Install** to download

To Update your apps

- Tap on the menu icon at the top left corner

- Tap on **My apps & games**

As shown below

You will be able to update your apps and games here. Also you can carry out some other activities like **payment, subscription, settings** and more in the menu list.

Tips & Support

As shown below

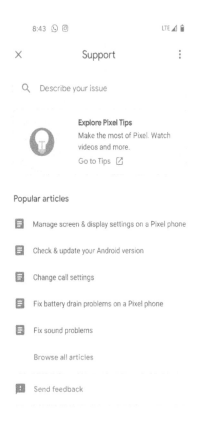

You can fix your device sound problems, and battery here. Also you can search for some of your complaints here too.

Thanks for Reading

Although I have put in efforts to write this guide, and tips and tricks on the Google Pixel 5a 5G.

I have no doubt that I have not written everything available on the Google Pixel 5a 5G.

However, I will appreciate if you can send me an email on **sodiqtade@gmail.com** anytime you are unable to perform some task written in or outside this guide concerning the new Google Pixel 5a 5G.

I will try as much as possible to reply you as soon as I can.

Thanks for reading.

Made in the USA
Middletown, DE
16 June 2022

67265210R00086